CIRENCESTER
IN OLD PHOTOGRAPHS
FROM THE GLOUCESTERSHIRE LIBRARY
COLLECTION

CIRENCESTER

IN OLD PHOTOGRAPHS

FROM THE GLOUCESTERSHIRE LIBRARY COLLECTION

COLLECTED BY

JEAN WELSFORD

ALAN SUTTON
1987

Alan Sutton Publishing Limited
Brunswick Road · Gloucester

First published 1987

British Library Cataloguing in Publication Data

Cirencester in old photographs.
1. Cirencester (Gloucestershire) —— History
I. Welsford, Jean
942.417   DA690.G6

ISBN 0–86299–387–3

Typesetting and origination by
Alan Sutton Publishing Limited
Printed in Great Britain
by Redwood Burn Limited

CONTENTS

INTRODUCTION

Cirencester is changing. Over the last few years the town's population has grown, housing and commercial developments have proliferated and the volume of traffic in the streets has multiplied. Through these photographs something of the appearance and the life of the town as it was in the hundred or so years from the reign of Queen Victoria to the accession of her great, great grand-daughter, our present Queen, is recreated. Those who have long associations with the town, will, it is hoped, take pleasure in reviving memories of its past. Others who, like me, have grown to love it after a comparatively short sojourn, will perhaps enjoy an opportunity to deepen their acquaintance. Cirencester has been fortunate in its photographers who have captured with skill and affection the scenes and people of the past and preserved them for the future. Examples of the work of many notable nineteenth and early twentieth century photographers have been included, ranging from the intriguing Cox collection of Victorian inhabitants, possibly produced by T.W. Gough, to studies by Mortimer Savory, the sensitive, gifted amateur J.H. Thomas and the renowned Dennis Moss. Later photographers, thankfully, have continued their tradition and some of their work forms part of this selection.

All the photographs in this book have been taken from the Bingham Library Collection and I am indebted to Mr Bernard Stradling, the Gloucestershire County Librarian and Mrs Maureen Thompson, Librarian of the Bingham Library for their help and co-operation in this enterprise. The important Thomas collection is in the charge of the Bingham Library Trustees, now the Cirencester Town Council and I am very grateful to them for their kindness in allowing some of the pictures from this to be used.

SECTION ONE
The Market Place

THE MARKET PLACE photographed by J.H. Thomas in 1912. At the beginning of the nineteenth century there were three lanes at the top of the Market Place – Shoe Lane, Butter Row and Botcher Row – with a number of houses and shops. Beyond these, in what is now the open space between Rackham's and the King's Head, stood the Shambles and the 'blind' house or lock-up. The lanes and these buildings were demolished in 1830. One of the shops originally in Butter Row was that of John Smith, the chemist. His descendants continued in business till after the First World War on the site to which he removed after 1830. This is shown by the Chemist sign towards the bottom left of the photograph. The premises are now occupied by the National Westminster Bank.

THE MARKET PLACE has always been the natural focus of the Cirencester community. Here is a gathering outside the Church on an unknown occasion. It could possibly be the disbanding of the Cirencester 'D' Company of the Second Volunteer Battalion of the Gloucestershire Regiment in 1896.

THE MARKET PLACE decorated for the home-coming of Earl and Countess Bathurst after their honeymoon in 1893.

THE CORN HALL opened in 1862 on the site of the former Boothall where once the wool markets were held. The architects were Nedland, Nedland and Naberly. The Corn Hall Buildings opened in 1863 and eventually housed the Library and Subscription Rooms and the School of Art as well as the weekly Poultry and Butter Market.

CHARLES BINGHAM, eldest brother of Daniel Bingham, the founder of the Bingham Library, who for almost forty years had a confectioner's and pastry cook's business in the shop adjacent to the Corn Hall where Barclay's Bank now stands.

BISHOP'S STORES occupied an important position on the corner of the Market Place and Cricklade Street. The Bishop family were associated with the business from 1827 until 1914 when it was sold to make way for the Midland Bank.

These shops adjoining the King's Head and the old Market Hall were pulled down at the end of the nineteenth century and replaced by the Wilts and Dorset Bank.

ALEXANDER AND PUMPHREY whose ironmonger's shop is seen here, had another outlet and a foundry in Cricklade Street. The gabled building is the White Hart Inn, pulled down in 1872.

THE MARKET PLACE looking towards Jefferies' Corner. The gables of the White Hart are visible. The town pump, often a favourite rendezvous, was still in use at this time. Cirencester had no piped water supply until after 1882 when the Waterworks Company was founded.

GREENWOOD'S, House Furnishers, (later W. Saunders) stood on the site of the White Hart. In recent times, Timothy White's, now succeeded by Carpenters, was here.

THE MARKET PLACE. A view of the North side showing the magnificent porch added to the Parish Church of St John the Baptist about 1500. The photograph is undated but is certainly before 1881 since the tailors Hamper and Hiscock had been replaced by Hamper and Fry by then on the evidence of the 1881 census returns. Just visible at the extreme right edge is the long established business of Baily's, later Baily and Woods. This opened in 1835 and continued for 150 years, closing in 1985.

THE MARKET PLACE – a close-up of two well-known businesses. The tailor Hamper and his partner Fry have moved next door since the previous photograph on Page 16. Waldron Griffiths, the chemist, moved from the other side of the Market Place in 1892. This business was taken over by Hortons in the 1920s under which name it still trades.

THE MOP, held in the Market Place until recently, now takes place in the Forum Car Park. Once a traditional hiring fair, from the later years of the nineteenth century it became an amusement fair only. It is held on the two Mondays which fall either side of old Michaelmas Day (10 October), unless 10 October is a Monday in which case there will be three Mops instead of two. This photograph shows the scene in 1930.

THE MOP, another view of 1930. Notice the steam coming from the steam roundabouts. At one time steam engines were forbidden because of the noise.

THE SUN INN — a seventeenth-century inn shown here with its original façade which was altered in the nineteenth century. The Sun closed in the 1920s and was then for some time the garage of Messrs H. Tovey and Son.

A VIEW FROM THE MARKET PLACE looking towards Dyer Street, taken in the early years of this century. The fishmonger's shop of F.W. Moody can be seen on the right of the picture next to that of 'Honest Joe' Matthews, the tobacconist.

Town and Around
1. Town

DYER STREET – about 1912. The offices of the Wilts and Gloucestershire Standard are seen with their frontage recently rebuilt by local builders, Saunders. The printing works at the back, extending into Lewis Lane were occupied in the pre-railway era by the warehouses and stables of Tanner and Baylis, the carriers. On the right can be seen the houses built by Earl Bathurst in 1889 to replace the old gabled cottages which formerly stood there.

THE BULL INN, Dyer Street, taken in 1913. The adjoining cottages were pulled down to make way for Steel's Garage in the 1920s.

THE BULL INN, A close-up view, also showing a typical alleyway with several cottages hidden away from the street

WEST MARKET PLACE — taken just before Castle Street was widened in 1897, and Jefferies' Corner put back to its present position. Messrs Hyde's draper's shop is now the Edinburgh Wool Shop.

WEST MARKET PLACE — Jefferies' Corner with the Ram Inn beyond. The Ram was once a famous coaching inn with an entrance in the Market Place. It declined with the coming of the railways and finally disappeared in 1897 when new buildings replaced the block in Castle Street from Jefferies' to the junction with Silver Street.

CASTLE STREET. The Great Western Refreshment Rooms. Before 1897 these stood on the site of the present Post Office, enticing weary travellers on their way to and from the railway station in the Tetbury Road.

CASTLE STREET — The Globe Temperance Hotel. Obviously supported by local temperance reformers, this too occupied a good position for attracting travellers. The hotel porter presumably has either returned or is about to leave for the station with a guest's luggage.

CASTLE STREET. The handsome Lloyd's Bank building was originally a wool merchant's house dating from the early eighteenth century. About 1790 it was taken over by Pitt, Bowly and Croome as the premises for their bank. On the right the garden railings of Elm Court are just visible.

CASTLE STREET. Elm Court, pulled down to make way for Castle Buildings, once belonged to the Bowly family.

CASTLE STREET. These buildings were erected in 1897. The Post Office then moved to its present site from further down Castle Street. The Urban District Council Meetings were transferred from the Town Hall to the new Municipal Office in the centre of the block. The Council continued to meet here until 1932 when it moved to Gosditch Street.

CASTLE STREET. Viners — an established business from the beginning of this century. This photograph is from an undated collection, entitled 'Beautiful Britain'.

CASTLE STREET in late 1920s or early 1930s. Legg's Shop on the left is part of Castle Buildings which replaced Elm Court. The Gainsborough Studios were owned by Dennis Moss, the well known Cirencester photographer. He took over the studios from Mortimer Savory, another local photographer of repute.

CASTLE STREET, looking towards the Tetbury Road. The building in the distance is the Town Museum erected by Earl Bathurst in 1856. The Hairdresser's and Umbrella shop belonged to John Kittow.

JOHN KITTOW who ran the hairdresser's shop pictured above. A well-known Cirencester character, he was born in 1818 in the Shambles and died in 1916 aged 97. At one time he was Town Crier.

CASTLE STREET. The site of John Beecham's painting and decorating business is now the office of Cirencester Benefit Society. John Beecham moved here from 15 Park Street, (Dunstall House) in 1865 and the premises remained in his family until 1912.

JOHN BEECHAM, 1813 – 1882. In addition to his decorating business, John Beecham was well known as a painter of romantic historical Cirencester town scenes. He was also an accomplished signwriter, heraldic artist and lithographer. A staunch and outspoken Liberal, he was a member of the Cirencester Local Government Board from 1876 until his death in 1882.

KENNET JOHN BEECHAM, 1848–1922. John Beecham's eldest son. Educated at Cirencester Grammar School, he followed a career as an architect and civil engineer, spending a large part of his life in London. In 1887 the Wilts and Gloucestershire Standard published his *History of Cirencester*.

CASTLE STREET. This fine timbered house, now part of W.H. Smith's, was converted into a garage by Bridges at the beginning of this century. Adjoining are the dilapidated premises of Paish, a brush and broom dealer. The family of Paish were known in the town as basket makers over many years.

CASTLE STREET. W.H. Smiths took over from Bridge's Garage in the 1920s. Beyond is the Black Horse which today incorporates another former public house – the King's Arms. This operated until 1924.

CASTLE STREET, showing Farrell's Cycle Shop. Mr Farrell's father had shops on the other side of the street and the family is remembered in the new Farrell Close which leads into Brewery Court from Castle Street.

CASTLE STREET. Farrell's Stores was a well-known shopping landmark. Who could resist the offer of 10,000 articles at 5½d each?

CASTLE STREET. A photograph of the rest of Farrell's Stores. Mr Farrell, the gentleman in the bowler hat, moved to Castle Street after his premises, 'The Little Dustpan' in Gosditch Street were destroyed in a disastrous fire in 1880.

CASTLE STREET. Astons, the jeweller's shop is now part of Messrs Scotts, gentlemen's outfitters. The lady standing outside is Mrs Jane Aston.

CASTLE STREET. A window display of Scotts, the outfitters, showing the prices of a bygone age!

CASTLE STREET. The Bell Inn at the junction with Cricklade Street, now the premises of Hobbs and Chambers, Estate Agents.

CRICKLADE STREET. A photograph taken about 1915 just before Bishop's was pulled down.

CRICKLADE STREET. Part of the Brewery Offices. These buildings date from the early 1890s.

CRICKLADE STREET. The Brewery Staff, taken in the early 1930s. Brewing ceased at the Cirencester Brewery in 1937 when it was bought by H & G Simmonds.

CRICKLADE STREET. Alexander and Thompson's Wholesale ironmongers department where Woolworths now stands. It was later taken over by J.H. Cock, who, in partnership with a man called Bartholomew, owned a carriage and coach building works.

MR & MRS H.J. ALEXANDER. Henry Alexander was the founder of the firm, later known as Alexander and Pumphrey, then Alexander and Thompson. He also operated a successful foundry in Cricklade Street. A keen temperance supporter, he opened a Working Men's Club in his premises in 1867.

CRICKLADE STREET. Buncombe's later took over the premises once occupied by Alexander and Thomas and ran a similar business.

CRICKLADE STREET – The Bishop Blaize Public House before 1892 when the road was widened and the front of the building put back. It was probably named after St Blaize, the patron saint of Woolcombers whose craft flourished in the town during the height of the wool trade.

CRICKLADE STREET. Shilham's, the Butchers. This adjoined the Bishop Blaize and after the road widening in 1892 also had its front altered and put back. Mr Shilham took over from John Peckham in 1910, maintaining the tradition, only recently broken, of a butcher's business on the site since at least 1792.

44

CRICKLADE STREET. The famous 'dog-leg' bend, widened in 1892. Before then the street narrowed here to a width of 12 feet. This was one of the main routes to both railway stations, and with two-way traffic, there was often congestion and danger to pedestrians. Jackson's – a well-known ironmonger and edge-tool maker – can be seen at the left of the picture.

CRICKLADE STREET. The Rose and Crown Public House at the bottom of the street. One of the many public houses now closed. Henry Cuss and his wife, Rose, are standing outside.

CRICKLADE STREET. A view from the Lewis Lane/Querns Lane crossroads. Note the railings outside Nos 74 and 76 which have long since disappeared. The store of Cock and Bartholomew, carriage makers, is visible. The board over the alley way advertises Frederick Pearce, chimney sweep.

CRICKLADE STREET. John Smith's other premises at the junction with West Way. The frontage was later altered but the business was carried on here until the 1970s.

CRICKLADE STREET. John Smith was a corn and seed merchant of longstanding in the street. These premises are almost opposite the Ashcroft Road turn and were originally a public house called the Salutation, later the Fox, which closed in the 1870s.

CRICKLADE STREET. Ashcroft House — A large family home, surrounded by seven acres of orchards, pasture and pleasure gardens. Sold by the Cripps family to Earl Bathurst in 1847, it was occupied by a number of tenants until 1890 when William Cripps re-purchased it. Six acres were sold as building land and Ashcroft House and the remaining acre survived until the 1960s when it too was demolished for further housing development.

CRICKLADE STREET. Ashcroft House. One of the tenants in the 1860s was Major Milligan, a retired Life Guards' Officer. He had a small daughter, Mary, aged five in 1861. This photograph was probably taken in the grounds of Ashcroft House.

CRICKLADE STREET/LEWIS LANE. A photograph of the Bathurst almshouses taken just before the First World War.

QUERNS LANE. The home of the Brewin family in the latter part of the nineteenth century. The Brewins were prominent local Quakers and philanthropists.

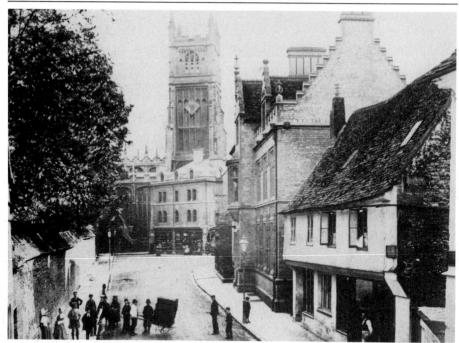

GOSDITCH STREET – 1880. The shop obscuring the view of the Church is the Little Dustpan, destroyed by fire later in the same year. The new Capital and Counties Bank building completed in 1876 can be seen on the right. In the twentieth century this became the offices of the Cirencester Urban District Council.

WEST MARKET PLACE. Old London House. A postcard of 1911, showing the building, later demolished to widen the road and clear the space by the Church.

WEST MARKET PLACE. A photograph taken about 1911, showing old London House and Burrows advertising Clearance Sales. Plans were being made at this time to pull down these shops. The butcher's business of Tranter later moved to Castle Street.

BLACK JACK STREET, about 1864–5. The house with three gables on the right was the birthplace of Daniel George Bingham, founder of the Bingham Library and Bingham Hall.

Silver Street, Cirencester.

SILVER STREET, probably a view from the early years of this century. The shop at the corner was known as a fancy repository and was kept by the Misses Marsh.

GOSDITCH STREET. An undated photograph showing two of the town's postmen. The timber-framed pair of shops survives today.

DOLLAR STREET in April 1914 – a view not substantially changed today.

Park Street & Vicarage, Cirencester.

PARK STREET. The first house which can be seen on the left of the picture is Monmouth House, said to date from the fourteenth century and restored in the Tudor period. Beyond, on the same side is the three-storeyed eighteenth-century building, once the vicarage.

COXWELL STREET, with its narrow thoroughfare and so many genuine seventeenth and eighteenth century buildings that this street still retains something of the atmosphere of former years. The railings of the Baptist Chapel are just discernible. This was rebuilt in 1856/7 on the site of a much earlier foundation.

COXWELL STREET — Coxwell Court, now called Woolgathers, is a seventeenth and early eighteenth-century house built around a courtyard. In the nineteenth century it was at one time the home of a branch of the Hoare family, important wool staplers. The warehouse which they used was around the corner in Thomas Street.

Gloucester Street, Cirencester.

GLOUCESTER STREET. A view of the street at the turn of the century, showing various types of transport, including a tricycle!

THOMAS STREET. The Weavers' Hall, founded by Sir William Nottingham who died in 1483, for poor weavers in the town. Beyond in Dollar Street can be seen Legg's grocery store.

GLOUCESTER STREET. Sheppard's Place in 1912. The date over the entrance is 1694. This is a surviving example of the alleyways and courts in which some of the past inhabitants of the town lived. The pillar on the right is Roman, presumably incorporated when the premises were built.

SHEEP STREET. Cottages photographed years before the new ring road was constructed in the 1970s. The building at the end, on the corner of Querns Lane, was the Hope Inn.

CECILY HILL. A nineteenth century view. The Tontine buildings, on the right, completed in 1802, have recently been renovated.

CECILY HILL. The Barracks, sometimes called The Armoury. Built in 1856 these were used to house the North Gloucestershire Militia, later the Fourth Battalion of the Gloucestershire Regiment, when they came to the town for their annual training.

Town and Around
2. Around

AN AERIAL VIEW DOWN BLACK JACK STREET to Cirencester Park beyond. The Mansion, home of Earl and Countess Bathurst, has been known at various times in its history as Oakley Grove, Apsley House and Cirencester House. It is normally hidden by the great yew hedge and is not open to the public. The Park was first landscaped in the eighteenth century by the first Earl Bathurst, assisted by his friend, the poet, Alexander Pope.

CIRENCESTER HOUSE, here called Apsley House, a nineteenth century photograph. Apsley is a family name of the Bathursts, originating from the marriage of the first Earl with his cousin Catherine Apsley. The original house on the site was built by Sir John Danvers in the late sixteenth or early seventeenth century. The first Earl altered this and later in 1830 another wing was added.

CIRENCESTER PARK – The Broad Ride – a nineteenth century view of the famous avenue which stretches five miles to the Golden Valley, Sapperton.

CIRENCESTER PARK – Pope's seat situated at the junction of the Seven Rides. Alexander Pope was a frequent visitor at the time of the first Earl, and was very interested in the planning of the Park which included the building of a number of follies, a characteristic of the period.

CIRENCESTER PARK – Alfred's Hall, sometimes known as the Woodhouse, was one of the follies built by the first Earl, and is of significance today as one of the earliest, if not *the* earliest of the castellated follies which became so popular. It was sometimes the venue for local concerts, picnics and other activities. This group is probably made up of cadets of the Cirencester Volunteer Rifle Corps.

ALLEN ALEXANDER, SIXTH EARL BATHURST who inherited the title from his uncle, William Lennox, the fifth Earl, in 1878. He built the Cirencester Cottage Hospital in memory of his first wife, Meriel, daughter of Baron de Tabley, in 1875.

COUNTESS BATHURST, second wife of the sixth Earl, before her marriage, Evelyn, daughter of George James Bernard Hankey.

ABBEY HOUSE. This was built in 1776 to replace the Tudor Mansion erected by Dr Richard Master when he purchased the site of the former Augustinian Abbey from Elizabeth I in 1564.

The Abbey, Cirencester. From S. W.

ABBEY HOUSE – another view of the house, which was pulled down and replaced by a development of flats after part of the Abbey Estate was sold to the Cirencester Urban District Council in 1965.

COLONEL THOMAS WILLIAM CHESTER-MASTER, who inherited the Abbey Estate from his father in 1899, having previously managed it for a number of years. He died in November 1914.

MRS CHESTER-MASTER, wife of Colonel Chester-Master, before her marriage, Georgina, daughter of J.W. Rolls Esq. of Hendre in Monmouthshire.

THE ABBEY GROUNDS — haymaking — A peaceful scene captured just before the First World War.

A VICTORIAN GROUP photographed in the surviving Norman gateway of the Abbey. The gentleman on the extreme left is Colonel Chester-Master.

THE BEECHES. Now the home of the Phoenix Community Centre, the house dates from the early nineteenth century and was once occupied by Mr Baylis who, with Tanner, operated an extensive carrying service. In the hall still exists the carved mantelpiece with a representation of an old Fly Waggon and team of eight horses similar to that used by Baylis and Tanner on their trade cards. The house was later in the hands of the Sewell family for many years.

THE BEECHES – a later ninteenth-century picture after the front had been altered.

EDWARD CLARE SEWELL. A local solicitor and High Steward of the Borough, he was keenly interested in the history of the town and its preservation. It was Edward Sewell who presented the Cox collection to the Bingham Library in 1923, from which this photograph and others in this book have been taken.

THE BEECHES. A group of servants at the house in the nineteenth century.

THE QUERNS. Built for Charles Lawrence and his wife Lydia (née Bowly) in 1825 on land leased to him by the third Earl Bathurst. The house in now incorporated in the Querns Hospital Complex.

The New Mills, The Beeches, Cirencester.

NEW MILLS, the Beeches. These were built by the last Abbot of Cirencester, in the sixteenth century. They continued to be used as cloth mills until the early nineteenth century and then as flock mills by the Ebsworth family. The Mills were demolished in 1912 but the Mill House survives.

NEW MILLS. An interior view a few years before demolition.

The Barton, Cirencester.

THE BARTON. Built on the site of a Roman Villa, the house dates originally from the seventeenth century, but has since been restored. At one time it was the home of Robert Alexander Anderson, a nineteenth-century agent to Earl Bathurst.

BARRETT – a maid at the Barton in the last century.

View on the Churn, Cirencester

Cecily Series

PEACEFUL SCENES along the River Churn.

THE TOWN – A bird's eye view from the Barracks on Cecily Hill.

Education and Entertainment

THE OLD GRAMMAR SCHOOL in Park Lane. Reputedly founded by John Chedworth, Bishop of Lincoln in 1458, the Grammar School started life in Dyer Street and moved to Park Lane probably at some time in the sixteenth century.

THE GRAMMAR SCHOOL, Victoria Road. The School moved here in 1881 with Revd G.R. Faulkener as Headmaster. Following a government report of 1869 a decision was taken to found an Upper School for Boys, incorporating money from the Powell's Trust with the Grammar School income. Today the building is used by the Cirencester County Junior School.

THE REVD WILLIAM BARTRAM. He was appointed as assistant master in 1846 and later became Headmaster. During his term the school numbers declined. In 1869 the school was reported to be out of repair with 25 day pupils and seven boarders, three of whom had not returned three weeks after the holidays!

POWELL'S SCHOOLS, Gloucester Street 1912. Part of the original yellow school buildings. The plaque, barely visible in the photograph, bears an inscription stating that the school was endowed by Rebecca Powell in her will in 1722 but that it opened in 1740. The long interval was caused by a legal dispute. The Yellow School catered for 40 boys and 20 girls. The Blue School in Gloucester Street, founded in 1714 for 20 boys and 20 girls, was also endowed by the generosity of Rebecca Powell and her husband, Thomas.

POWELL'S SCHOOL, showing the Victorian additions. Today these are partially hidden behind the 1987 extensions. The Blue and Yellow Schools were amalgamated in 1876 as Powell's School.

In the South wall of the Parish Church can be seen this painted figure of a Blue School Boy which used to stand in the porch to encourage donations for the Blue and Yellow Schools.

SOME OF THE PAST PUPILS OF THE BLUE AND YELLOW SCHOOLS. The boys' dress consisted of a cap, brass-buttoned coat, vest, knee breeches and stockings of yellow or blue, with leather buckled shoes. The girls wore dresses and tippets and bonnets trimmed with blue or yellow ribbon. On special days a frilled cap, shown in the photograph, was worn instead of a bonnet.

PUPILS OF CHARLES GREEN who in the nineteenth century ran the private school – the
Cotteswold Middle Class School at Linden House.

WATERMOOR NATIONAL SCHOOL. This Church of England School, founded in 1853 was originally for girls and infants only.

THE ROYAL AGRICULTURAL COLLEGE. These buildings were opened in 1846, having been erected by local builders Thomas Bridges. Until they were ready, two houses were rented in Thomas Street for the first students – 25 in all.

A group of boys from the Council or Board Schools which opened in Lewis Lane in 1879. The headmaster (seated) was Mr Harrison. The photograph is undated.

Another group from the same school also undated but obviously later than the photograph above.

SIR CHARLES BROOKE AND HIS SONS. Sir Charles Brooke (Rajah Brooke) lived at Chesterton House for a number of years. His family were first associated with the government of Sarawak through Sir Charles' uncle, Thomas. Sir Charles' son Vyner, shown here, was the last white Rajah of Sarawak.

CHESTERTON MUSEUM. Sir Charles Brooke was a great collector and opened his private museum, shown here, to the public. It remained open some time after his death in 1917 but finally closed in 1920.

MAJOR WILFRID CRIPPS. He was a member of a well-known local family prominent in the town's affairs from the eighteenth century. A keen archaeologist, he located and partially excavated the Roman basilica in 1898. His collection of Roman antiquities was housed in a purpose built museum at his property in Thomas Street and later bequeathed to the Corinium Museum.

COUNTESS BISMARCK, Mrs Wilfrid Cripps. She shared her husband's enthusiasm and interests and carried on his work after his death in 1903.

DANIEL GEORGE BINGHAM, 1830–1913. He was the founder of the Bingham Library and the Bingham Hall. Born in Cirencester in Black Jack Street, as a young man he was employed as a clerk at the G.W.R. Station in the town. He moved to Paddington and in 1855 went to Holland with James Staat Forbes when the latter was appointed to re-organise the Dutch–Rhenish railways. Three years later, at the age of 28, Daniel Bingham succeeded Forbes as General Manager. He made a substantial fortune from investments and although when he retired in 1890, he made his home in Utrecht, he was a generous benefactor to his native town.

THE OPENING CEREMONY OF THE BINGHAM LIBRARY on 21 September 1905 in the Market Place. The Library was actually opened by Hon. William Bathurst whose second birthday it was.

THE BINGHAM LIBRARY — The original site shown here was once the Bull Inn and afterwards a cheese factor's warehouse. By this date (1903) it was a depot for an omnibus company.

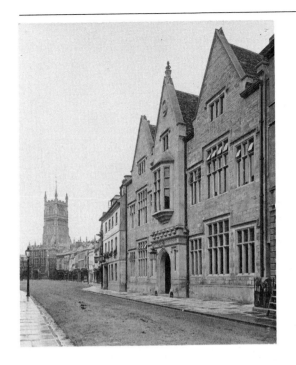

THE BINGHAM LIBRARY. The completed building. The architect was V.A. Lawson and the total cost of the operation was about £50,000. Of this, £28,000 was invested to provide for the services of a professional librarian and staff. The Library today houses the offices of Cirencester Town Council.

THE BINGHAM LIBRARY. The entrance hall and central staircase. The staircase was built of stone and the landing windows were fitted with stained glass from Amsterdam, a reminder of Mr Bingham's Dutch associations.

THE BINGHAM LIBRARY. Ladies' Sewing Group. Needlework classes were held on Mondays and Thursdays during the winter months. The cost of tuition was met by Daniel Bingham. During the First World War the classes were incorporated into a branch of Queen Mary's Guild of Needlework.

THE BINGHAM LIBRARY in later days. A view of the Lending Library, by this time on the ground floor. Mr Peter Jackson, the Librarian who retired in 1970, is seen attending to a reader.

THE BINGHAM LIBRARY. A view of the Reading Room in the 1950s.

THE BINGHAM LIBRARY. A school visit.

AMATEUR THEATRICALS 1887. Amateur Theatricals were an important part of entertainment in Cirencester in the nineteenth century and the tradition continued into the present period. The name of the piece which this group performed has not been recorded on the photograph but the players' names are known. Standing from left to right they are: F.W. Woods, E. Phillips, A.E. Bartlett, F. Hoare, J. Matthews, Miss Beauchamp, W. Parry, H. Gardner, Miss Gobey, — Allen and A. Ovens. Seated from left to right: Miss Beauchamp, Miss T. Delaval, T.B. Shenton, Miss L. Henderson, Miss I. Hart.

THE MISSING DUKE — performed at the Bingham Hall in 1909. This photograph was taken behind the Hall, and houses in Victoria Road are discernible in the background.

THE ROYAL PAVILION PIERROT PARTY, 1896. One of the performances given by the Amateur Dramatic and Operatic Company associated with Cirencester Cricket Club. Sydney Boulton, seen on the right of the photograph, was a founder member of both. The other players are Mrs Stradling, A. Stradling and F.M. Savory.

DONE ON BOTH SIDES — A farce performed at the Apsley Hall, Sheep Street in 1893. From left to right: Sydney Boulton, Wilson Tovey (seated), F.W. Woods, Miss S. Allen, Miss K. Allen.

F.W. Woods as Svengali and Sydney Boulton as Trilby in *A Trilby Fantasy* at the Corn Hall in 1896. Sydney Boulton was a member of the Boulton family who had a long established draper's business where Rackhams is now. F.W. Woods was in partnership with Baily in the Market Place Bookseller and Printers, and took over the business in 1896 but continued to trade under the old name.

CIRENCESTER DICKENS FELLOWSHIP IN "MR PICKWICK"

Two splendid performances of " Mr. Pickwick," as adapted from the Pickwick Papers, by Councilor H. O. Barnett, of Chelte were given before crowded audiences at the Bingham Hall Cirencester, by members of the Cirencester Fellowship.

Standing, from left: Augustus Snodgrass (Mr. H. Lea), Nathaniel Winkle (Mr. H. T. Lock), Mrs Weller (Mrs. R. J. Benney), Weller (Mr. F. P. Cox), a landlady (Mrs. R. H. Bailey), Mr. Wardle (Rev. F. W. Parkinson), Mary (Miss Wall), Sam W (Mr. H. J. Legg), a buxom female (Mrs. K. T. McHugh), Mr. Stiggins (Mr. J. Bosworth).

Sitting, from left: Joe, the fat boy (Mr. F. N. Cole), Mrs. Wardle (Miss M. Paish), Mr. Perkins (Mr. J. Hall), Emily Wardle J. Beeny), Mr. Pickwick (Rev. T. C. Simpson), Isabella Wardle (Miss C. Keane), Tracey Tupman (Mr. R. Parr), Rachael W (Miss C. Crook), Alfred Jingle (Mr. L. Harrison).

"Cheltenham Chronicle" Photograph. Copies 1s. and 1s. 9d. each.

THE DICKENS' FELLOWSHIP, 1934. An account of a performance from the *Cheltenham and Gloucester Graphic.*

AN IDEAL HUSBAND, performed in the Bingham Hall by Ciceter Drama Club, 1950.

BRITISH LEGION PAGEANT. Narrators from a pageant held in Cirencester Park in the 1950s.

THE BEECHES BARN PLAYERS. In 1948 The Beeches was purchased for use as a Community Centre. The Barn Theatre was opened in 1950 and the Beeches Players' first performance in the new theatre was *The Confutation of Wisdom*.

Sports and Associations

CRICKET IN CIRENCESTER PARK. The Cirencester Cricket Club was formed in 1842 and played in Cirencester Park. On occasions it was strong enough to beat an all England XI.

A CIRENCESTER CRICKET XI.

A GROUP OF NINETEENTH CENTURY CRICKETERS.

CIRENCESTER GOLF CLUB began in 1893 at Park Corner, Sapperton. The present Golf Course was opened in 1910.

THE V.W.H. MEET. Boxing Day 1888. The tradition of the meet on Boxing Day still continues but no longer in the Market Place. Today this takes place on the lawns of the Mansion in Cirencester Park.

A GROUP OF INTREPID SWIMMERS at the Open Air Swimming Pool. The Pool dates from 1870 when the Swimming Bath Company was formed to provide Swimming Baths for the town. These are still in use today.

ROLLER SKATING in the Corn Hall just before the First World War.

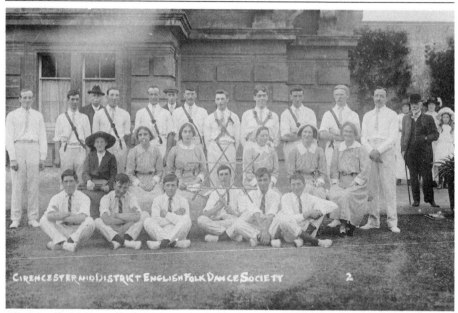

CIRENCESTER AND DISTRICT ENGLISH FOLK DANCE SOCIETY – date unknown.

STRATTON FOLK DANCE CLUB 1912. The lady second from the left is Miss May Cambray.

COUNTY BOWLS MATCH AT CIRENCESTER

In fulfilment of a promise made at the annual dinner of the Cirencester Bowling Club the first county bowls match was played on the Cirencester green at Ashcroft last week-end. The match was between Gloucestershire (who won by 17 shots) and Herefordshire.

1.—Mr. F. Withy (Stroud) bowling.
2.—A view of the pretty green, with the match in progress.
3.—Mr. E. Ford (Exmouth) bowling.

4.—Cheltenham players, who were included in the county team.
5 and 7.—Friends of the players watching the match.

6.—Spectators. At back are three lady players who came, thinking it was a ladies' match.
8.—Mr. F. W. Gibson, Mr. E. A. Greenslade, Mr. E. R. Howard and Mr. T. C. Boulton (all of Cirencester).

" Cheltenham Chronicle " Photographs. Copies 1s. and 1s. 9d.

A COUNTY BOWLS MATCH at Cirencester Bowling Club, Ashcroft 1934.

GENERAL VIEW OF THE HALL, WITH JUDGING IN PROGRESS.

CIRENCESTER FUR AND FEATHER ASSOCIATION. This photograph is of the annual show in 1908 in the Bingham Hall. The first members' show was held in 1896.

Church and Chapel

THE PARISH CHURCH OF ST JOHN THE BAPTIST. A photograph of a print of the Parish Church from the 1830s showing the organ above the Chancel arch before it was removed to its present position in later nineteenth century restoration work.

THE PARISH CHURCH OF ST JOHN THE BAPTIST. A view of the graveyard in snow. This was in use until the new cemetery at Chesterton was opened in 1871.

WILLIAM POWELL, Vicar of Cirencester 1839–1869. While William Powell was vicar the restoration work on the Parish Church by Sir George Gilbert Scott was completed 1865–7.

WATERMOOR CHURCH. This was designed by Sir George Gilbert Scott and consecrated in 1851. The spire was added in 1852, at the expense of the Hon. William Lennox Bathurst, afterwards the fifth Earl Bathurst.

ARCHDEACON SINCLAIR. Vicar of Cirencester 1898 – 1909.

The Combined Choirs of Cirencester Parish Church and Watermoor Church in 1903.

THE CHURCH CHOIR — on their annual outing — on this occasion in 1914 they went to Cheddar.

THE BOYS' BRIGADE. The first Cirencester Company. Another pre-First World War photograph.

CHURCH LADS' BRIGADE. Trooping the colour in the Abbey Grounds.

CHURCH LADS' BRIGADE. At camp at Dawlish in 1912.

THE CONGREGATIONAL CHAPEL, Dyer Street. This was pulled down in 1971 and replaced by Waitrose Supermarket. It had been built as a substitute for the Congregational Chapel in Sheep Street which became the Cirencester Memorial Hospital.

WHARF ROAD CHAPEL CIRENCESTER.

THE INDEPENDENT OR CONGREGATIONAL CHAPEL, Sheep Street. A photograph of an early print of the Chapel which was built in 1839. Sheep Street is called Wharf Road here because of its proximity to the Canal.

THE REVD JOSEPH STRATFORD, Minister of the Congregational Chapel for a number of years, in the nineteenth century. He was also known for his biographical studies, *Good and Great Men of Gloucestershire,* and *Wiltshire and its Worthies.*

STRATTON CHURCH. The Lych Gate.

ASHCROFT METHODIST CHURCH. This was founded in 1896 when the sale of the Ashcroft Estate allowed development in this part of the town. The entrance until recently in Ashcroft Road, has now been moved to the side of the building in Ashcroft Gardens.

Public Services

CIRENCESTER FIRE BRIGADE — horse-drawn — outside the Kings Head. On the front of the engine is Captain Hibberd. Back Row: F.J. Saunders, Arthur Tranter, William Knapp, W. Mills, Charlie Protherough. Front Row: George Hulbert, Fred Hulbert, Fred Guest, Henry Day, Fred Organ, Charlie Price.

CIRENCESTER FIRE BRIGADE 1918 – photographed outside the Barracks on Cecily Hill. The C.U.D.C. purchased the motor engine in 1914. Fire services were re-organised in 1918 when the Cirencester Brigade became part of South Western Area four. Seated beside the driver is the captain Mr A.J. Matthews, later Chairman of the C.U.D.C. He had a cycle manufacturing business in Cricklade Street.

CIRENCESTER POLICE STATION AND MAGISTRATES' COURT. This building on the corner of Castle Street and Park Lane opened in 1859. Before this, the police station was at a house in Gloucester Street and the Magistrates' Court was held in the Town Hall.

COTTAGES PULLED DOWN IN CASTLE STREET to make way for the new police station in 1859.

POLICE SUPERINTENDENT EDWIN RIDDIFORD. He took charge of Cirencester's police force in the 1850s.

THE WAGGON AND HORSES in the London Road. This photograph dates from 1913. Horse-drawn transport was still widely used at this period. Many people from surrounding villages were dependent on local carriers and carters for getting themselves and their goods to and from Cirencester.

CIRENCESTER AND FAIRFORD DISTRICT BUS. This shows the bus outside the Bull Hotel at Fairford. These were the early days of motor transport and the journey from Fairford to Cirencester took from fifty minutes to an hour.

THE TOLL HOUSE AND GATES AT STRATTON. The present road to Cheltenham was opened in 1827 and was turnpiked. Users paid a toll at the toll house for the privilege. After the ending of the turnpike system, the former toll house was resited further up the Cheltenham Road.

THE THAMES – SEVERN CANAL – CIRENCESTER WHARF. This photograph dates from 1904. For the first time for many years a narrow boat has arrived with a load of coal. The Canal had declined because of competition from the railways and in 1882 an Act of Parliament allowed the Great Western Railway to take up an option to purchase it. The Canal Wharfhouse seen in the background was pulled down in 1975 in the construction of the ring road.

FRANK GEGG, operated from the Wharf from the last decades of the nineteenth century until the early 1920s. A number of coal merchants continued to use the wharf but many of their supplies now came by road and rail.

FRANK GEGG AND 'JOEY'.

A VIEW TAKEN FROM THE QUERNS, just before the First World War, showing the yards and sidings of the Great Western Railway.

OUCESTERSHIRE RAILWAY STATION STAFFS. No. 7.—CIRENCESTER G.W.R. STATION.

Standing :—W. Waters, F. J. Smith, C. Brown, J. Evans, F. Coates, H. Morgan, F. Uzzell, F. Wood, F. Jay, F. Pritchard, Eyles, F. Hayward, C. Mills, J. Alsopp, F. Selby, E. Jones, C. Stephens, J. Drew, E. Evans, H. Rowberry, H.G. Page, B. Hyett. Seated :—W. Allen, C. Feldwick, F. C. Fagent, F. E. George (stationmaster), A. Couldrey, S. E. Dike, "David" Richards o was stationed at Cirencester G.W.R. Station for 36 years, and who was recently presented with a silver watch and purse of ney from his colleagues and Cirencester tradesmen), and T. Lane.

STAFF AT THE G.W.R. STATION AT CIRENCESTER. The railway opened as a branch line to Kemble in 1841, linking Cirencester with London and the south west. It closed in 1966.

CIRENCESTER COTTAGE HOSPITAL. This was built by the sixth Earl Bathurst in 1875 in memory of his first wife.

RED CROSS HOSPITAL, THE BINGHAM HALL. This opened in December 1914 with 80 beds. Wounded men were brought to the Hospital from the nearby Watermoor Station.

People and Events

BLONDIN IN THE PARK. The famous French high-wire acrobat visited Cirencester in 1892.

M. SALMET, the French aviator gave an aerobatic display in aid of the Cirencester Cottage Hospital in 1912. Photographed with him in the Abbey Grounds are Major and Mrs Dugdale, tenants of Abbey House, and Master Eric Dugdale.

THE BACHELORS' CLUB, enjoying a river trip.

THE BINGHAM HALL – laying the Foundation Stone by Countess Bathurst, 7 March 1908. The Hall was presented to the town by Mr D.G. Bingham.

THE BINGHAM HALL — The opening ceremony performed by Mrs D.G. Bingham, 14 October 1908.

A VICTORIAN WEDDING GROUP. The bride was Miss Sealy and the bridegroom was Mr Hodges.

This photograph bears the label, LADY MERIEL BATHURST AND LORD APSLEY as children. They were the eldest son and only daughter of the seventh Earl and Countess Bathurst. Lord Apsley, father of the present Earl, was killed on active service in 1942. Lady Meriel Bathurst married Lord Alistair Graham, a younger brother of the Duke of Montrose, and died at a comparatively early age in 1936.

AUGUSTUS WHATELEY, aged 100. One of Cirencester's oldest inhabitants who lived at Watermoor.

CIRENCESTER CADET CORPS. Part of the Cirencester Volunteer Rifle Corps (Second Volunteer Gloucestershire Regiment) which was disbanded in 1896.

CIRENCESTER NATIONAL RESERVE. Church Parade, December 1912. 126 Reservists mustered at the Bingham Hall and marched to the Parish Church, accompanied by the band of the Midland and South Western Junction Railway.

THE RESERVISTS outside the Church – December 1912.

An undated and unnamed photograph presumably taken during, or at the end of the First World War. Red Cross contingents are being reviewed in the Abbey Grounds.

ST JOHN'S AND RED CROSS VOLUNTEER NURSES from the First World War. Miss Constance Hadow is seated on the extreme right and Miss May Cambray is standing beside her.

A GROUP OF STRATTON A.R.P. WARDENS from the Second World War.

TENANTS OF THE ABBEY AND KNOLE PARK ESTATES. A gathering on the occasion of the coming of age of William Chester-Master in 1924. He had inherited the Abbey Estate and the other family estate of Knole at Almondsbury (Glos) when his father, Lieutenant-Colonel Richard Chester-Master, was killed on active service in France in 1917.

DOLLAR STREET, 1929. Widespread flooding in the town brought opportunities for unconventional means of transport!

DOLLAR STREET, 1929. Another photograph showing that at least some seemed to have enjoyed the situation.

THE HON. BEN BATHURST'S CAR well decorated during his successful parliamentary election campaign in January 1910. He defeated the Liberal candidate R.W. Essex by 983 votes.

A CARNIVAL FLOAT. This photograph, by P.G. Morse, is undated but may be from the 1920s when a branch of the League of Nations' Association flourished in the town. The Summer Carnival, in aid of the Cottage Hospital, was held in the Abbey Grounds at this period.

Royal Occasions

QUEEN VICTORIA'S GOLDEN JUBILEE, 1887. A view of the procession passing through the Market Place.

BICYCLE RACING IN THE MARKET PLACE. Part of the sports organised to celebrate the occasion. The bicycles are just discernible in the distance.

A CLOSE-UP OF ONE OF THE ENTRIES IN THE GOLDEN JUBILEE PROCESSION. Cirencester had raised £320 by public subscription to mark the Jubilee on 21 June. Events included church services, the procession, sports, tea for schoolchildren and a public dinner for 500 people in the Corn Hall.

QUEEN VICTORIA'S DIAMOND JUBILEE, 1897. A large crowd assembles as 10 years earlier. Note the horse-drawn fire engine stationed at the bottom of the Market Place ready to deal with emergencies.

GEORGE V'S ACCESSION, 1910. Proclaimed, as was usual on these occasions, in front of the Parish Church.

OX ROASTING AT WATERMOOR. One of several such events to celebrate George V's coronation.

THE PROCLAMATION OF QUEEN ELIZABETH II'S ACCESSION, in 1952.

THE LION AND THE UNICORN – Oliver Hill's 16ft ropework group was the spectacular centrepiece of the town's decorations to celebrate the Coronation of the present Queen in 1953. The supporting obelisks were in purple and white, topped with angelic trumpeters and red geraniums.

A CLOSE-UP OF THE CENTREPIECE.

THE DECORATIONS ILLUMINATED AT NIGHT.